P9-DES-782

GO QUIZ YOURSELF ON SCIENCE

IZZI HOWELL

CRABTREE
PUBLISHING COMPANY
WWW.CRABTREEBOOKS.COM

CRABTREE
PUBLISHING COMPANY
WWW.CRABTREEBOOKS.COM

Author: Izzi Howell
Editorial director: Kathy Middleton
Series editor: Izzi Howell
Editor: Crystal Sikkens
Proofreader: Wendy Scavuzzo
Series design: Rocket Design (East Anglia) Ltd
Prepress technician: Katherine Berti
Print coordinator: Katherine Berti

Every effort has been made to clear copyright. Should there be any inadvertent omission, please apply to the publisher for rectification.

The website addresses (URLs) included in this book were valid at the time of going to press. However, it is possible that contents or addresses may have changed since the publication of this book. No responsibility for any such changes can be accepted by either the author or the publisher.

All facts and statistics were correct at the time of press.

Picture acknowledgements: Getty: Maxchered 5, RobinOlimb 7t, ttsz 7b, cnythzl 21c, drmakkoy 32b, faegga 33b; Shutterstock: Mochipet, Laia Design Lab, NeMaria and ShadeDesign cover and title page (left to right), Drogatnev, EgudinKa, Alexander Ryabintsev, BSVIT, drvector, Abscent, VectorMine, Vecton and NeMaria 4 and 10–11, CRStocker, rehab-icons, Alfmaler, Sabelskaya and lady-luck 5, nalin chanthorn, Maquiladora, Sudowoodo, Spreadthesign and BlueRingMedia 6t and 10–11, Metelitsa Viktoriya, Auspicious and Ramona Kaulitzki 6b, Fancy Tapis 7c, trgrowth 8–9c, Pogorelova Olga 9t, Designua 9b, eHrach, ASAG Studio, Arizzona Design, Grinbox, NEGOVURA and Viktorija Reuta 12t and 16–17, anemad 12b, SkyPics Studio 13tl and 17, littleartvector 13tr, KannaA 13b, yusufdemirci 14t, Ilya Bolotov 14b, Lorelyn Medina 15t, Artur Balytskyi 15b, IfH 18t, Nadya_Art 18bl, ByEmo 18br, Skycolors 19t, Natali Snailcat 19bl, Marish 19br, grayjay 20t, NoPainNoGain 20b, ShutterStockStudio 21t, Snowbelle 21c, Volodimir Zozulinskyi, MSSA, VVadyab Pico and Portare fortuna 21b, reuse from 18–21 22–23, alazur, Ket4up, Aleksangel, Julia Lemba, bus109 and Topuria Design 24, Orakunya 25t, Vectors Bang 25b, VectorSun 26tl, DwaFotografy 26tc, VectorKnight 26tr, Nasky 26b, MicroOne 27t, Mironova Iuliia, SofiaV, pear worapan and miniaria 27b, reuse from 24–27 28–29, Kachalova Kseniia, VectorPlotnikoff, JuliarStudio, Sudowoodo, Sketch Master, Giuseppe_R, NotionPic and IMissisHope 30, Orakunya, Jakinnboaz, Mironova Iuliia, imaginasty and Sudowoodo 31t, Hein Nouwens 31bl, VikiVector 32br, Vecton 32t, Usenko Oleksandr, Yana Alisovna, Sarunyu_foto, Spreadthesign and Drogatnev 32–33b, Bogdan Wankowicz 33t, MarBom 33c, reuse from 30–33 34–35, huyangshu 36l, HelloArt 36r, Fouad A. Saad 37t, Zvereva Yana 37b, StrongPickles, Andy Frith, KirillKazachek, Pogorelova Olga, Kobsoft, Sergey Merkulov, paradesign, Yeti Crab, Tetiana Yurchenko, Olha1981, bilha Golan, NotionPic, Timur Zima and Julia Tim 38–39, reuse from 36–39 40–41, TatyanaTVK 42t, A Aleksii 42b, Unitone Vector 43t, Blan-k 43b. All design elements from Shutterstock.

Library and Archives Canada Cataloguing in Publication

Title: Go quiz yourself on science / Izzi Howell.
Other titles: Science
Names: Howell, Izzi, author.
Description: Series statement: Go quiz yourself | Includes index.
Identifiers: Canadiana (print) 20200358111 | Canadiana (ebook) 20200358189 | ISBN 9781427128737 (hardcover) | ISBN 9781427128799 (softcover) | ISBN 9781427128850 (HTML)
Subjects: LCSH: Science—Juvenile literature. | LCSH: Science—Problems, exercises, etc.—Juvenile literature.
Classification: LCC Q163 .H69 2021 | DDC j500—dc23

Library of Congress Cataloging-in-Publication Data

Names: Howell, Izzi, author.
Title: Go quiz yourself on science / Izzi Howell.
Description: New York, NY : Crabtree Publishing Company, 2021. | Series: Go quiz yourself | Includes index.
Identifiers: LCCN 2020046067 (print) | LCCN 2020046068 (ebook) | ISBN 9781427128737 (hardcover) | ISBN 9781427128799 (paperback) | ISBN 9781427128850 (ebook)
Subjects: LCSH: Science--Juvenile literature. | Science--Problems, exercises, etc.--Juvenile literature.
Classification: LCC Q163 .H69 2021 (print) | LCC Q163 (ebook) | DDC 500--dc23
LC record available at https://lccn.loc.gov/2020046067
LC ebook record available at https://lccn.loc.gov/2020046068

Crabtree Publishing Company

www.crabtreebooks.com 1-800-387-7650

Published by Crabtree Publishing Company in 2021

All rights reserved. No part of this publication may be reproduced, stored in a retrieval system or be transmitted in any form or by any means, electronic, mechanical, photocopying, recording, or otherwise, without the prior written permission of Crabtree Publishing Company.

First published in Great Britain in 2020 by Wayland
Copyright ©Hodder and Stoughton Limited, 2020

Published in Canada
Crabtree Publishing
616 Welland Ave.
St. Catharines, Ontario
L2M 5V6

Published in the United States
Crabtree Publishing
347 Fifth Ave
Suite 1402-145
New York, NY 10016

Printed in the U.S.A./012021/CG20201102

CONTENTS

The world of science → 4
Light → 6
Sound → 8
Go quiz yourself! → 10
Energy → 12
Electricity → 14
Go quiz yourself! → 16
Forces → 18
Magnets → 20
Go quiz yourself! → 22
Materials → 24
Solids, liquids, and gases → 26
Go quiz yourself! → 28
Living things → 30
Plants → 32
Go quiz yourself! → 34
Ancient science → 36
Amazing inventions → 38
Go quiz yourself! → 40
The future of science → 42
Answers → 44
Glossary → 46
Further information → 47
Index → 48

HOW TO USE THIS BOOK

This book is packed full of amazing facts and statistics. When you've finished reading a section, test yourself with questions on the following pages. Check your answers on pages 44–45 and see if you're a quizmaster or if you need to quiz it again! When you've finished, test your friends and family to find out who's the ultimate quiz champion!

THE WORLD OF SCIENCE

Science helps us to understand the natural world and the way it works. Scientists are constantly discovering incredible facts that make us see the world around us in a whole new light.

TYPES OF SCIENCE

We often divide science into three main categories:

Biology–the science of life and living things

Chemistry–the science of **elements** and compounds

Physics–the science of the way the physical world works

MANY DIFFERENT TOPICS ARE STUDIED IN EACH AREA OF SCIENCE

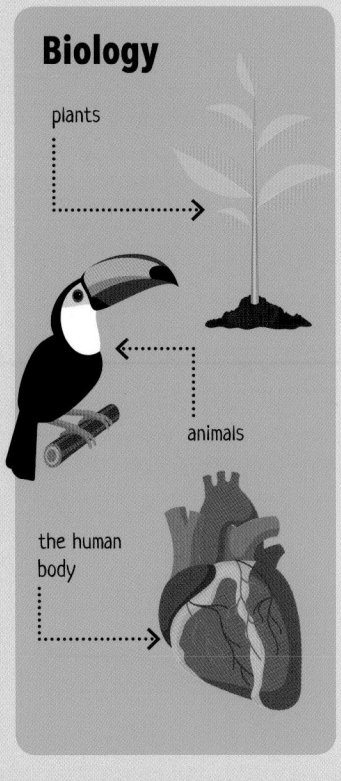

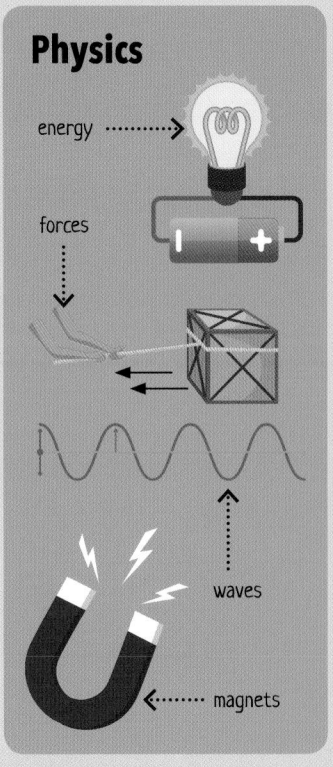

Water can exist as a solid, a liquid, and a gas

at the same time!

This can only happen in certain conditions at 32.018 °F (1 °C).

Find out more about solids, liquids, and gases on pages 26–27.

There is no sound in space!

This is because there are very few particles in space to vibrate, so sound waves can't travel.

Find out more about sound waves on pages 8–9.

Studying science has helped us to uncover some amazing facts.

There is enough electricity in the human brain when awake to power a

small lightbulb!

Find out more about electricity on pages 14–15.

Pancakes are usually round because of

GRAVITY!

The force of gravity pulls on the pancake batter evenly, forming it into a circle.

Find out more about forces on pages 18–19.

Some species of bamboo can grow up to

3 feet (1 meter) in one day!

Find out more about plants on pages 32–33.

SCORPIONS GLOW

in the light of a full moon!

Find out more about light on pages 6–7.

LIGHT

Light allows us to see objects. It reflects off objects and into our eyes.

LIGHT SOURCES

Objects that give off light are known as light sources. The Sun creates almost all of the natural light on Earth. We also use fire for light, for example, by burning candles. However, most of our light comes from human-made, electrical light sources, such as lightbulbs.

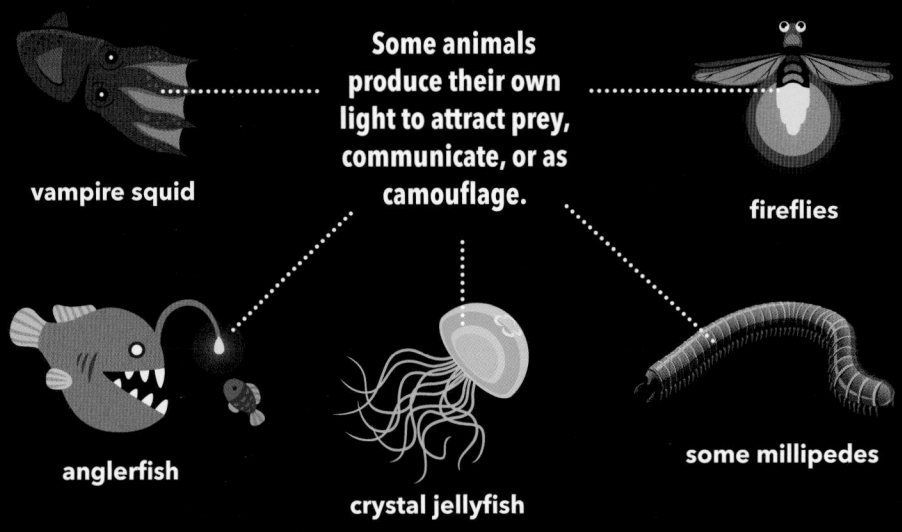

MATERIALS

Light can only pass through some materials. Transparent materials, such as glass, let light through. Translucent materials, such as colored plastic, let some light through. Opaque materials, such as wood, don't let any light through.

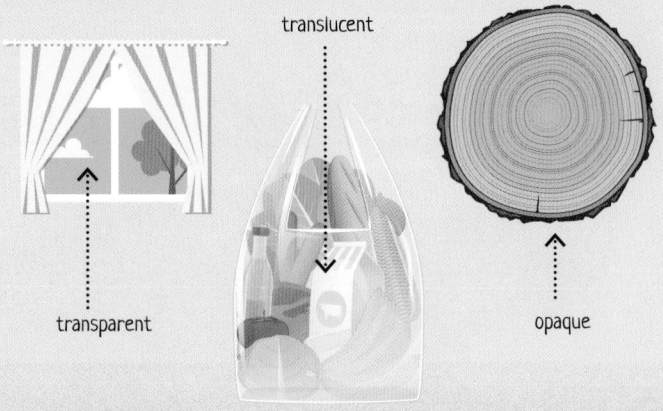

SHADOWS

When light is blocked by a translucent or opaque object, it creates a dark shadow behind the object. The size and shape of the shadow depend on the size and position of the light source.

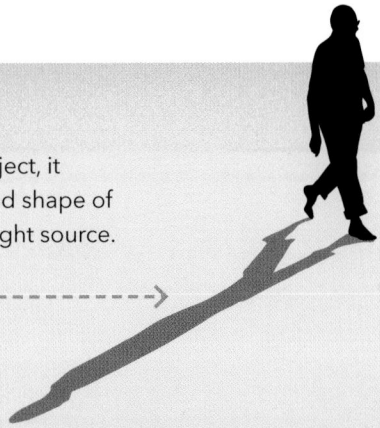

BENDING LIGHT

Usually light travels in straight lines, known as rays. However, rays of light can bend when they travel from one material to another. This is because they move more quickly through one material than the other. This is called refraction.

The bottom of the pencil appears to be in the wrong place. This is because the light bends as it moves between the air and the water in the glass.

SEEING COLOR

Light is a mixture of all colors. We see objects as colored because of the way the surface of the object reflects or absorbs the colors in light. If an object reflects all the colors of light, we see it as white. Some objects reflect just one color and absorb the rest. We see these objects as the reflected color, for example, red. If an object absorbs all of the colors, we see it as black.

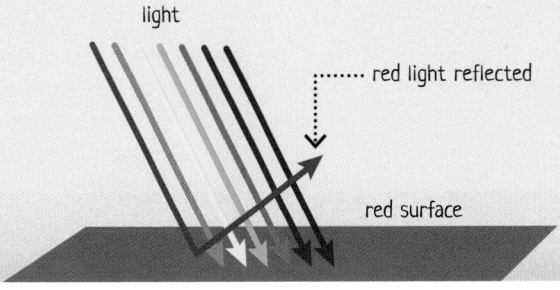

BIG, BLUE SKY

Air is transparent, but we see the sky as blue. This is because sunlight reflects off tiny particles in the air and gets scattered across the sky. Blue light is scattered more than other colors, giving the sky its blue color.

SOUND

Sound is created when objects vibrate, sending sound waves through the air. These waves enter the ear, where they are understood as sounds.

PITCH

Pitch is how high or low a sound is. The speed of the vibrations determines the pitch of a sound. Fast vibrations make high-pitched sounds, while slow vibrations make low-pitched sounds. Animals, such as dogs, have a wider range of hearing than humans and can hear sounds that we can't.

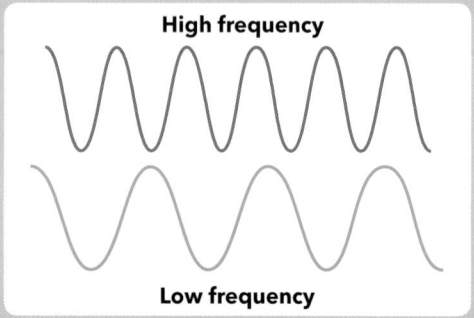

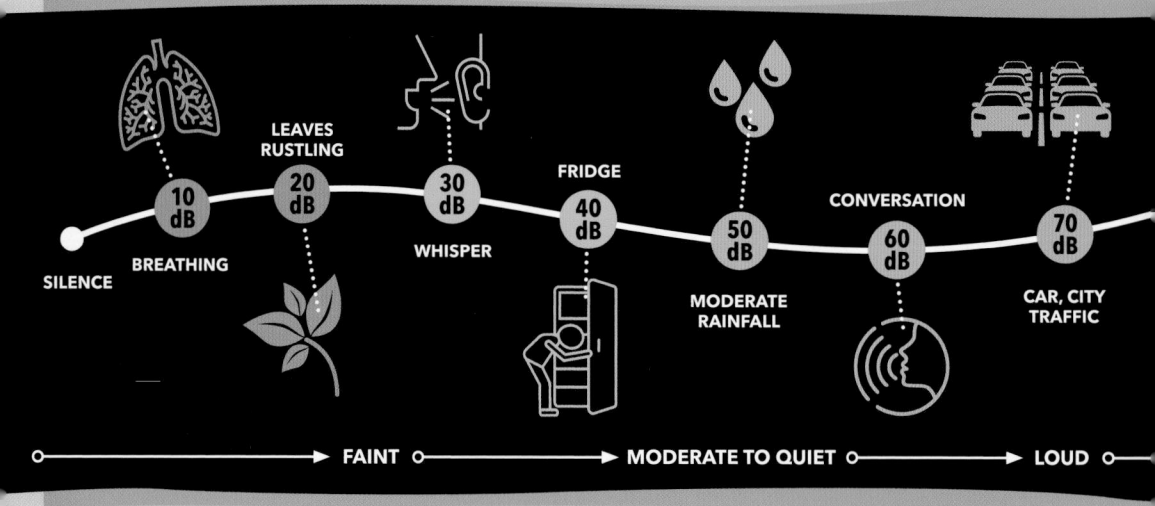

VOLUME

Volume is how loud something is. It is measured in decibels (dB). The taller a sound wave, the louder the noise. Loud sounds can damage the ear, so it's best to avoid them or wear ear protection in noisy situations, such as loud concerts or while using noisy machinery.

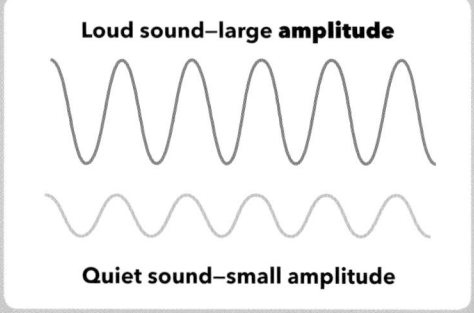

BOOM!

The loudest known sound on Earth was the eruption of the Krakatoa volcano in Indonesia in 1883. The sound registered an estimated 172 decibels at 99 miles (159 km) away, and the explosion was heard 2,175 miles (3,500 km) away in Australia!

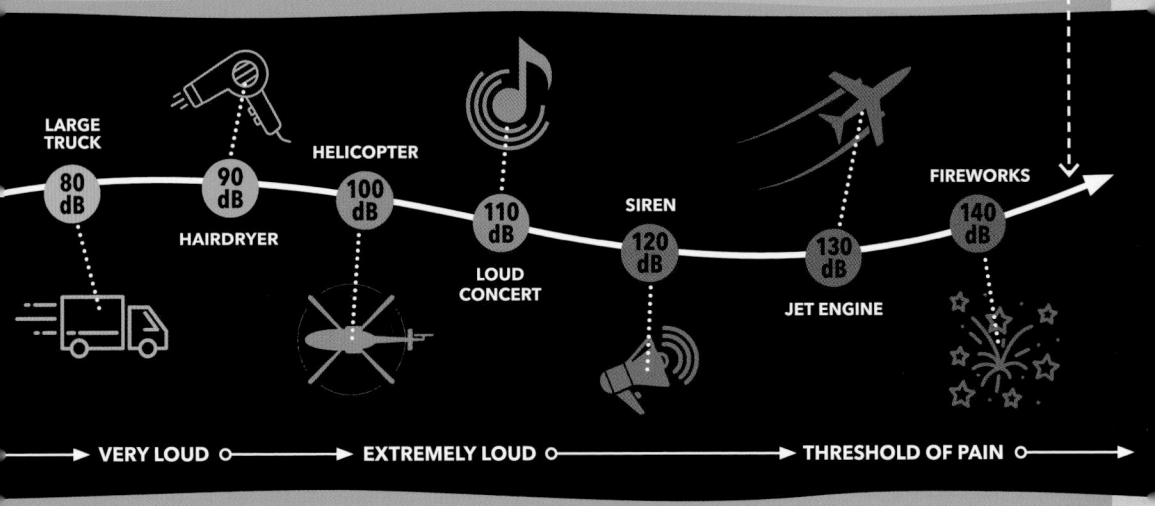

ECHOES

An echo is a repeated sound. Echoes are created when sound waves bounce off some objects and are reflected back to you so that you hear them again. Only hard objects create echoes, which is why they are commonly heard in tunnels or caves with hard walls. Soft objects absorb sound waves, so no echoes are heard.

Ships use echoes to find items underwater, such as fish. This system is called sonar. Ships send out sound waves that bounce off underwater objects. They use the reflected sound waves to know where the objects are.

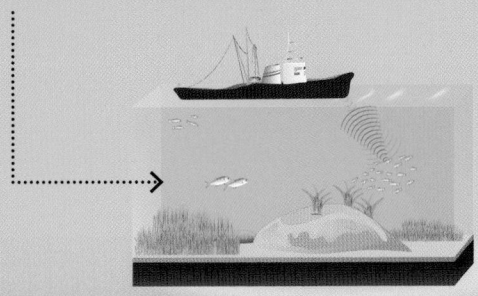

GO QUIZ YOURSELF!

1. What is studied in biology?
2. Which area of science studies magnets and energy?
3. Why are pancakes usually round?
4. Which animal glows in the light of a full moon?
5. What is a light source?
6. Name an animal that produces its own light.
7. Which word describes a material that doesn't let any light through?
8. When are shadows formed?

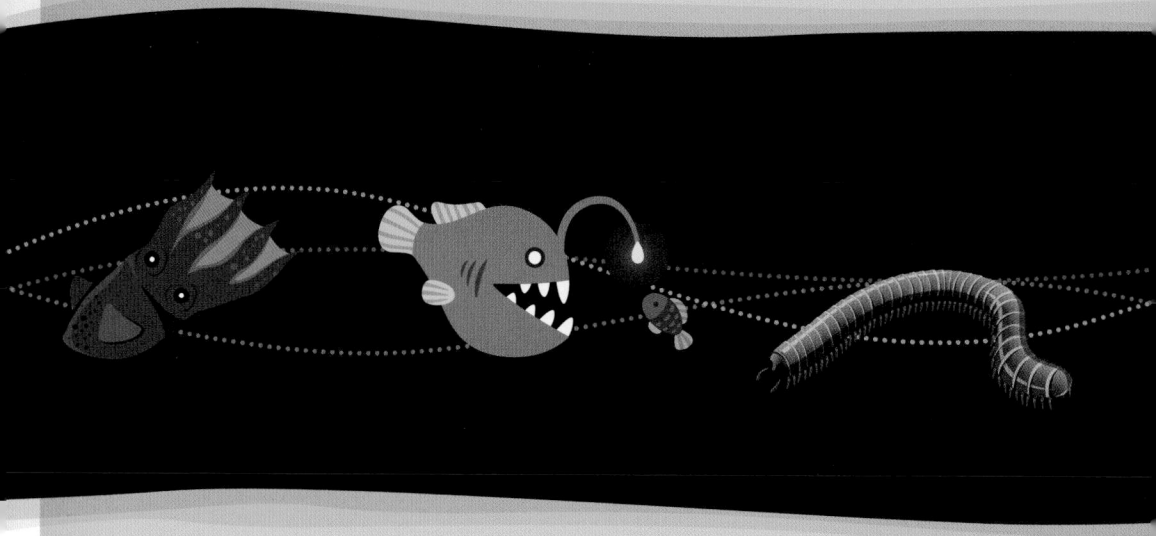

9. If an object absorbs all colors of light, what color do we see it as?
10. Why does the sky look blue?
11. If sound waves vibrate slowly, what pitch is the sound?
12. Who has better hearing—humans or dogs?
13. Which unit do we use to measure volume?
14. How many decibels is the sound of an average conversation?
15. What was the loudest known sound on Earth?
16. Why are echoes often heard in tunnels?
17. What is sonar?

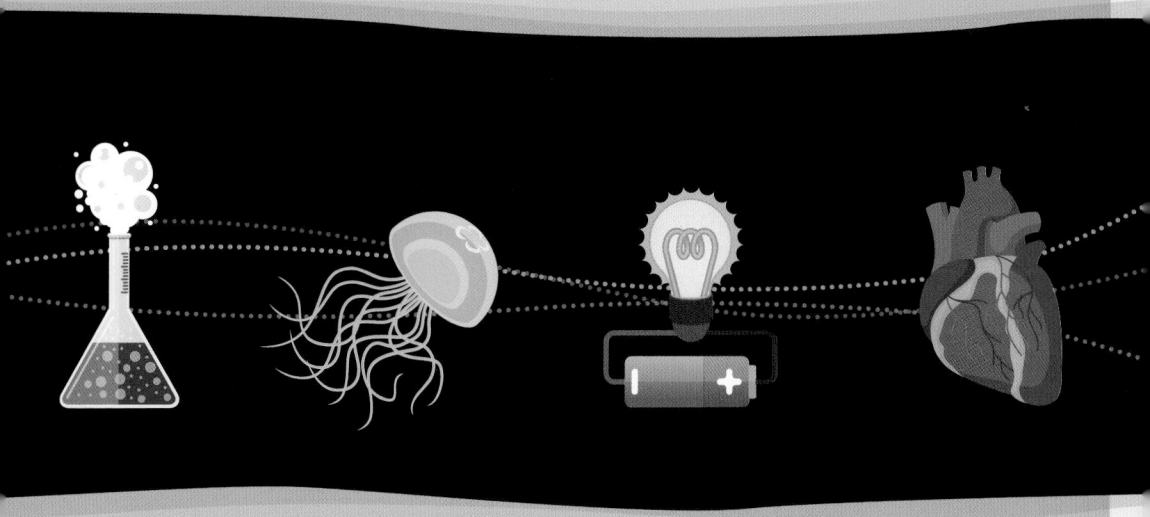

ENERGY

Energy makes things work. Every action requires energy, from moving and breathing to powering vehicles and machines.

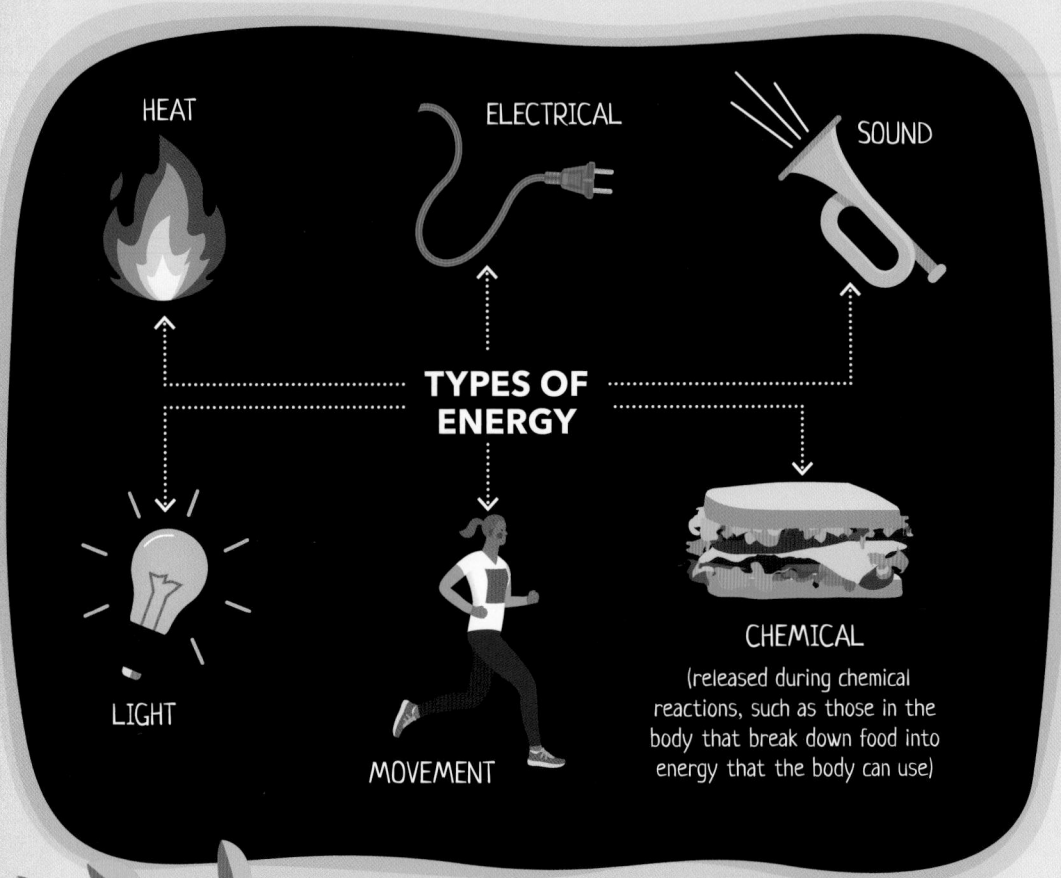

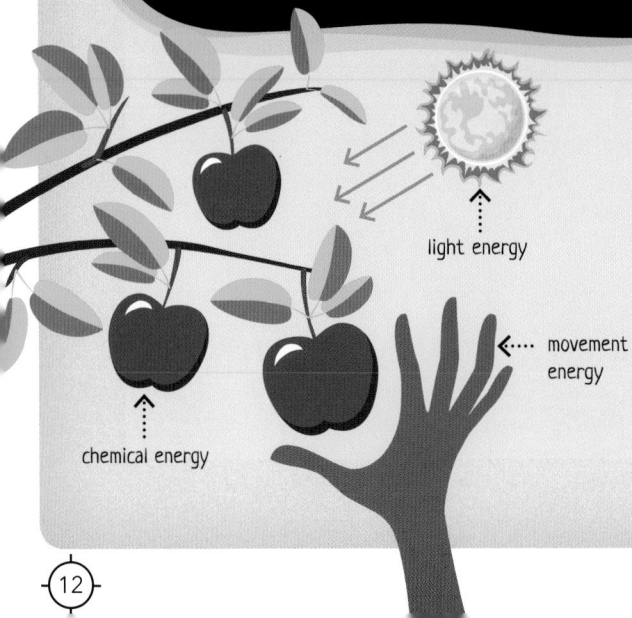

CHANGING ENERGY

Energy can be changed from one form to another. For example, electrical energy is turned into heat energy in a microwave or a toaster. Our bodies convert chemical energy from food into movement and heat to keep us warm. Plants turn light energy from the Sun into chemical energy (food).

GENERATING ELECTRICITY

There are several different ways of converting energy into electricity.

In fossil fuel power plants, chemical energy from fossil fuels is turned into heat energy when the fuels are burned. The heat energy is used to boil water, which creates steam. The steam spins a **turbine** (movement energy), which powers a generator that creates electricity.

In hydroelectric dams and wind turbines, movement energy from flowing water or wind spins a turbine, which powers a generator and creates electricity.

ENVIRONMENTAL PROBLEMS

Some energy sources create environmental problems. Burning fossil fuels creates air pollution and releases **greenhouse gases**, such as carbon dioxide. Greenhouse gases gather in the atmosphere and trap heat from the Sun close to Earth's surface. This increases the temperature on Earth (**global warming**), which disrupts natural habitats and changes weather patterns. Air pollution also leads to health problems, such as asthma and certain types of cancer.

GLOBAL WARMING

The average world temperature has increased about 2 °F (just over 1 °C) since 1880 because of **global warming**.

ELECTRICITY

Electricity is a type of energy. There are two types of electricity–current and static.

CURRENT ELECTRICITY

This type of electricity is found in **circuits** in buildings. It is used to power lights and appliances. Batteries also produce current electricity. A chemical reaction inside the battery generates the electricity.

CIRCUITS

A circuit is a path that electricity travels around, which is made up of wires and a source of electricity, such as a battery. Circuits can also contain other **components**, such as lightbulbs, motors, and buzzers. Switches are used to control circuits. A circuit has to be complete for electricity to flow around it. When a switch is open, it stops the flow of electricity around the circuit. When a switch is closed, the circuit is complete and electricity flows around the circuit.

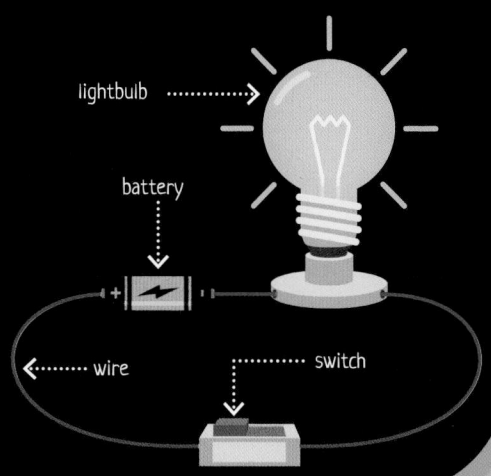

CONDUCTORS AND INSULATORS

Electricity moves differently through different materials. **Conductors** are materials that electricity passes through easily. Electricity does not pass through materials that are **insulators**. We use insulators to keep electricity safe. For example, plastic insulation on the outside of electrical wires stops the electricity from escaping.

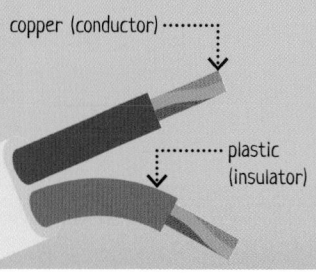

CONDUCTORS	INSULATORS
copper	plastic
iron	wood
steel	glass
water	rubber

STATIC ELECTRICITY

When two insulators rub together, tiny electrically charged particles called electrons jump from one material to the other. This build-up of electrons creates static electricity.

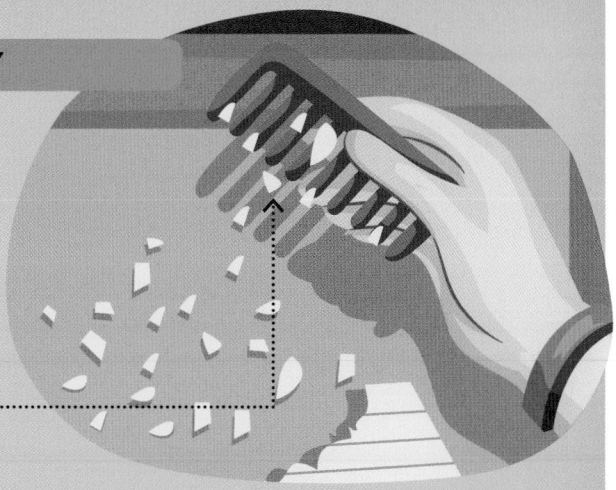

If you run a comb through your hair, it builds up a static charge and so the comb will be able to attract and pick up tiny bits of paper.

NATURAL ELECTRICITY

Electricity exists in nature. Lightning is static electricity that builds up in clouds. It is released down to the ground during storms. Animals, including humans, also generate electricity inside their bodies. A very small amount of electricity is used to send messages to and from the brain, and to make the heart beat. Some animals generate large amounts of electricity and use it to hunt and kill prey.

NATURAL ELECTRICITY

- ★ The longest-ever lightning bolt measured 440 miles (708 km), which is roughly the distance from Boston, MA, to Washington, DC.
- ★ The longest-ever duration of a lightning bolt was 16.73 seconds. The average duration of a lightning bolt is 0.2 seconds.
- ★ Lightning is five times hotter than the surface of the Sun.
- ★ Sharks have special electricity sensors on their skin. They use the sensors to detect the electrical signals in nearby prey.
- ★ Electric eels send out huge jolts of electricity to kill their prey.

GO QUIZ YOURSELF!

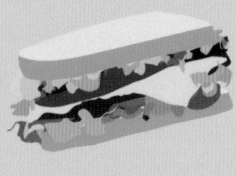

18. Name two types of energy.
19. What type of energy is food?
20. Describe the energy conversion that happens in a microwave.
21. Which two types of energy do our bodies create from chemical energy?
22. How is electricity generated in a hydroelectric dam?
23. What is a greenhouse gas?
24. Name a health problem caused by air pollution.
25. How much has the average world temperature increased since 1880?

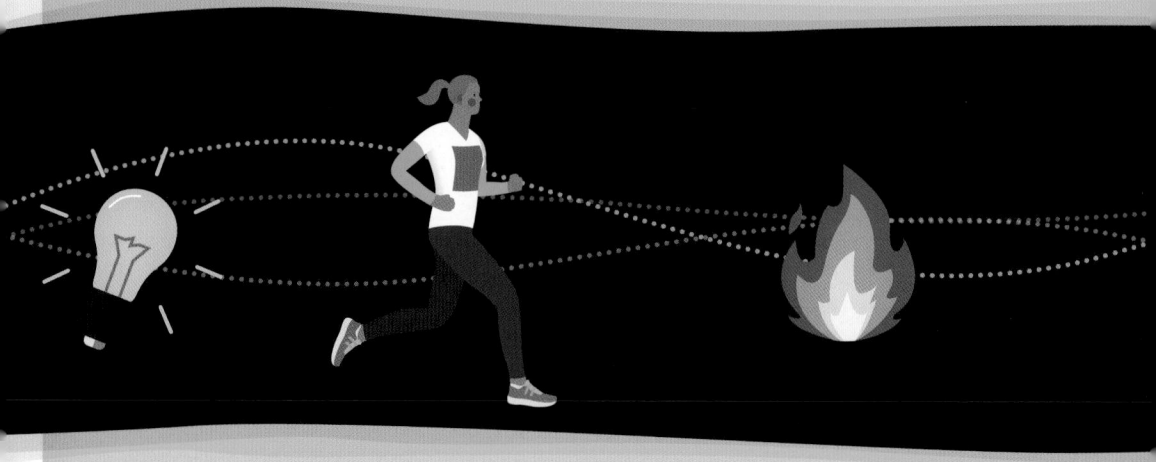

26 What are the two types of electricity?

27 Give an example of a component found in a circuit.

28 What happens to a circuit if its switch is open?

29 Name two materials that are electrical insulators.

30 What type of electricity is lightning?

31 How long did the longest-ever lightning bolt last?

32 Which is hotter—lightning or the surface of the Sun?

33 Name one way in which electricity is used in the bodies of most animals and humans.

34 Which animal uses electricity to kill their prey?

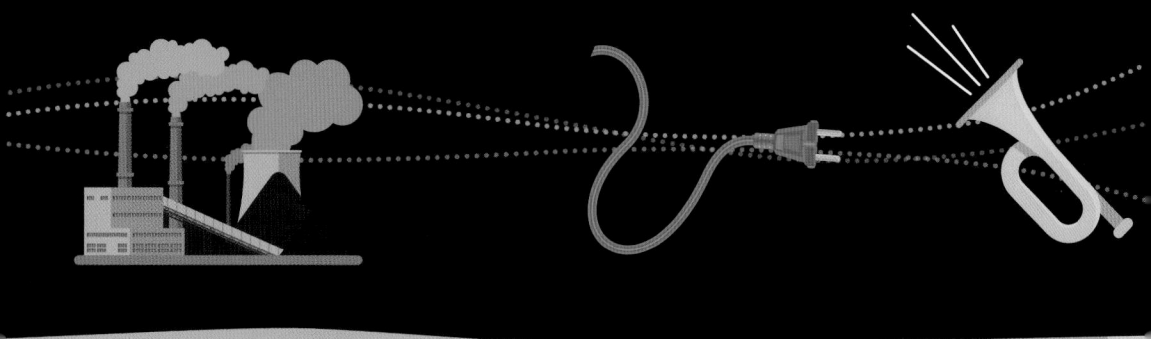

FORCES

Forces are pushes or pulls. They can make things move, change speed, change shape, and change direction.

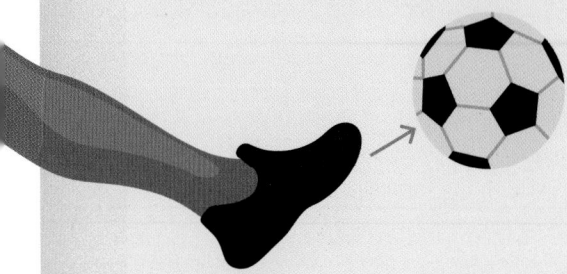

FORCES AND OBJECTS

The stronger a force, the greater an effect it will have on an object. Some objects need to touch for a force to have an effect, such as when a foot kicks a ball. Other forces, such as gravity, can affect objects without touching them.

FRICTION

Friction is the force that acts on an object when it moves against another object. It acts in the opposite direction to the movement of the object, which can make it hard for the object to move. Smooth surfaces have very little friction, while rough surfaces have more. Friction can be useful—it stops our feet from slipping on the ground.

GRAVITY

Gravity is a force that pulls objects toward each other. All objects have gravity, but heavier objects have more gravity than lighter ones. The heaviest object around us is Earth. Its gravity pulls everything else down to its surface. This is why objects fall to the ground if they are dropped.

RESISTANCE

When an object moves through air or water, it experiences **resistance** created by friction. This resistance slows the object down and makes it have to push harder to move through the air or water. The faster an object travels, the more resistance it experiences. **Streamlined** objects (those with a smooth shape) experience less resistance, and can move more quickly through air or water.

AIR FORCE

The thin shape of airplanes helps them to be streamlined.

The streamlined shape of airplanes helps them to move quickly through the air.

Horizontal wings help to keep the airplanes steady in the air.

Airplanes have a pointed nose to cut through the air.

Unstreamlined airplanes would require a lot of fuel to push them through the air, which wouldn't be energy- or cost-efficient.

BALANCING FORCES

If two forces of the same size act on an object in opposite directions, nothing will happen to the object. It will stay still or keep moving at the same speed. This is because the forces are balanced.

However, if one force is greater than the other, the forces are unbalanced. This means the object will move in the direction of the greater force.

The force created by the cyclist pushing forward is greater than the air resistance, so the cyclist moves forward.

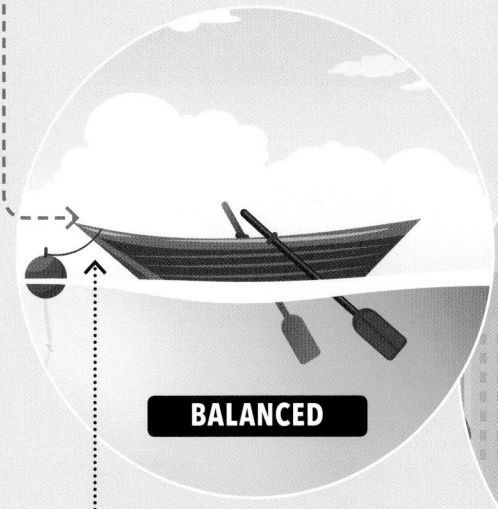

Boats float because the weight of the boat is balanced by the upthrust (pushing force) of the water.

MAGNETS

Magnets are objects that have an invisible force that pulls on magnetic materials from a distance. This force is called magnetism.

MAGNETIC OR NOT?

Magnetic materials are attracted to magnets, while non-magnetic materials are not.

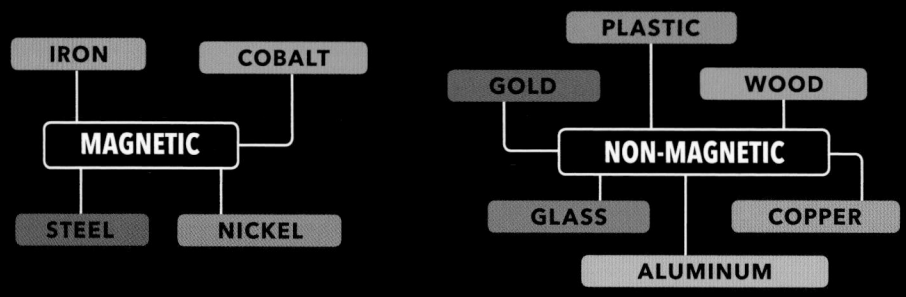

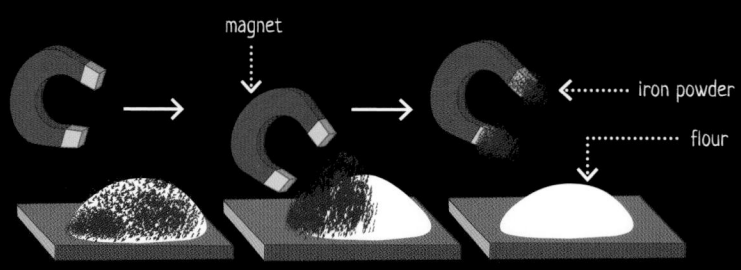

Magnets can be used to separate mixtures of magnetic and non-magnetic materials, such as this mixture of flour and iron powder.

POLES

The ends of a magnet are called poles. One end is the north pole and the other is the south pole. If you try to join two magnets together at the same pole, the poles will push away from each other or "repel." However, if you put two different poles together, they will attract each other and pull together.

Different poles attract

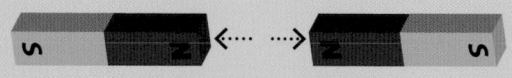

Same poles repel

MAGNETIC FIELDS

A magnet creates a **magnetic field** around it. This is the area that is affected by its magnetism. Magnetic fields are drawn as lines around a magnet. The closer the lines, the stronger the magnetic force. It is strongest at the poles.

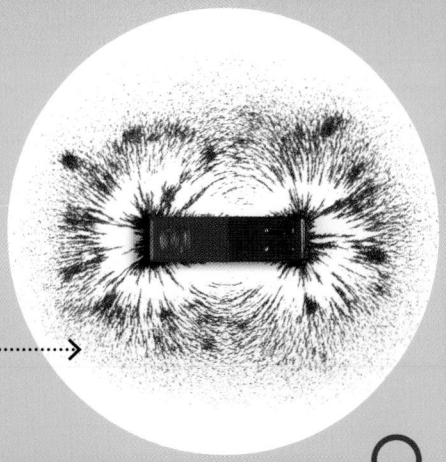

We can see the effects of a magnetic field for ourselves with iron filings and a magnet. The iron filings are attracted to the strongest areas of the magnetic field.

MAGNETIC EARTH

Earth is a magnet because it has magnetic materials, such as iron and nickel, in its core. Like any magnet, it has a north pole and a south pole. Earth's magnetic north and south poles are close to the geographic north and south poles (the most northerly and southerly points). We can use Earth's magnetic field for **navigation**, because compasses point to the magnetic north pole. Many animals, such as birds, can sense Earth's magnetic field and also use it for navigation.

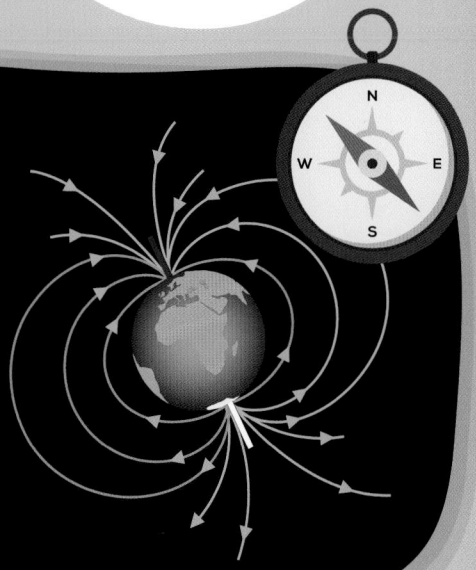

USES FOR MAGNETS

We can use magnets for many amazing things:

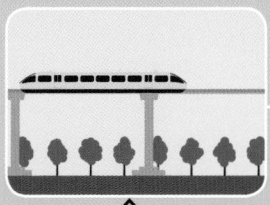

to hold high-speed Maglev trains above the tracks to reduce friction so they can move faster

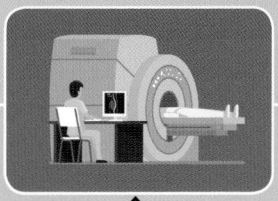

to look inside a person's body with an MRI machine to see if they are hurt or ill

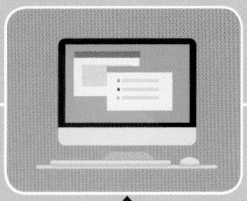

to store data in computers

to create sound in speakers and headphones

GO QUIZ YOURSELF!

35 Which force pulls objects toward each other?

36 Which objects have more gravity—light objects or heavy objects?

37 What is friction?

38 Why is it easy to ski across smooth ice and snow?

39 How does resistance affect the speed of an object?

40 What does "streamlined" mean?

41 Which part of an airplane helps to keep it steady in the air?

42 Why do boats float on water?

43 What happens to an object when the forces acting on it are unbalanced?

44 Name two magnetic materials.

45 What are the poles of a magnet?

46 What happens if you try to join two magnets together at the same pole?

47 What is a magnetic field?

48 Why is Earth a magnet?

49 Name a type of animal that uses Earth's magnetic field for navigation.

50 How do high-speed Maglev trains use magnets?

51 How are magnets used in computers?

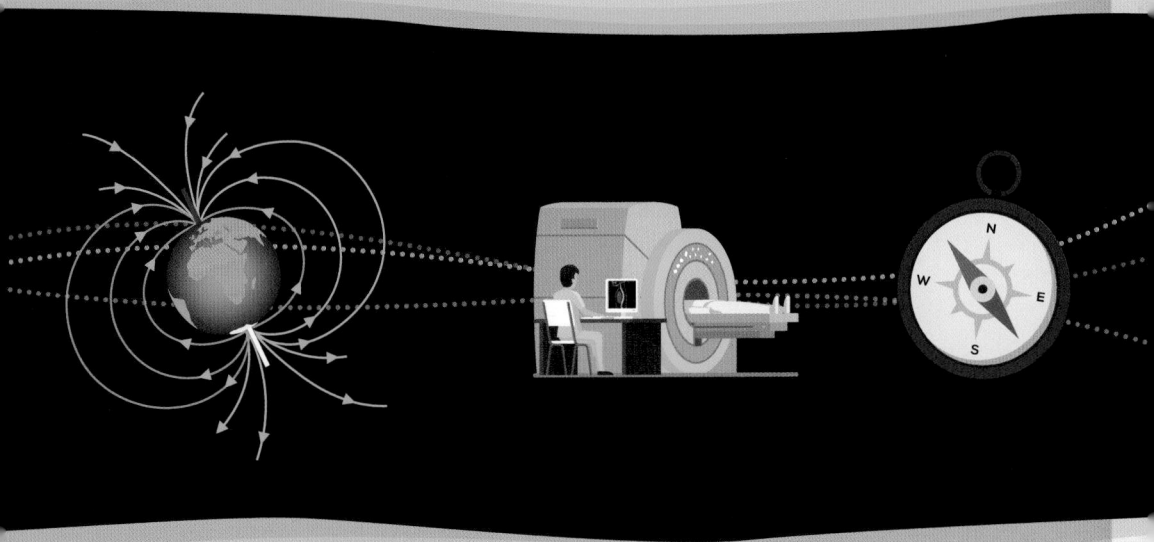

MATERIALS

Materials have different properties, such as being hard, soft, resistant, or fragile. A material's properties make it useful for certain purposes.

NATURAL AND HUMAN-MADE MATERIALS

We can divide materials into two categories: natural and human-made. Natural materials are taken straight from nature. Human-made materials are made by people from natural resources.

NATURAL

METAL (from the ground)

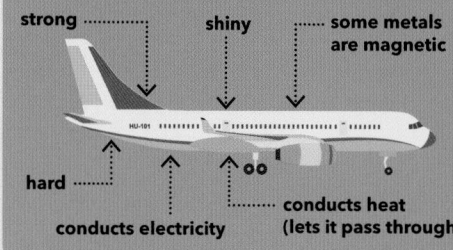

WOOD (from trees)

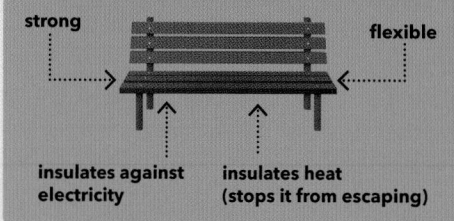

ROCK (from the ground)

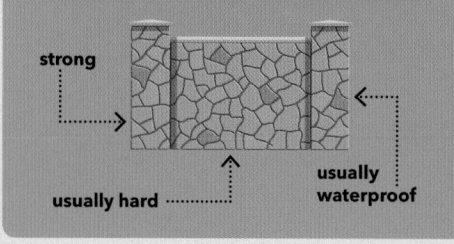

HUMAN-MADE

PLASTIC (usually made from chemicals found in natural gas and oil)

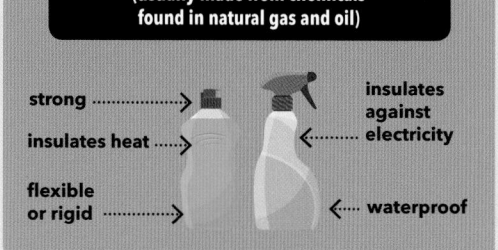

GLASS (made from sand and minerals)

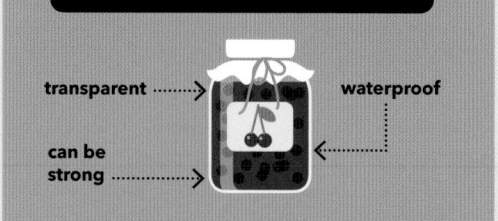

FABRIC (made from plant, animal, or human-made fibers)

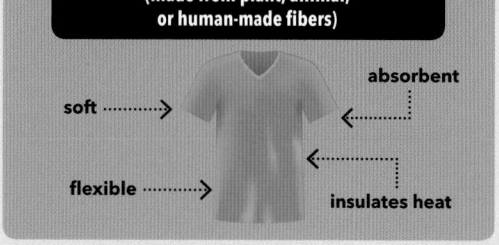

LONG-LIFE MATERIALS

Human-made materials, such as plastic, are often durable. They last a long time without breaking down. This can be useful, because we don't want some objects to be fragile or break easily. However, this is a problem when these materials are thrown away because they will not decompose for hundreds or even thousands of years. They often end up in the oceans or in landfill sites, polluting natural environments.

RECYCLING MATERIALS

Some materials can be reused or recycled. We can reuse the object as it is, or break down the material and reshape it into something else. This is good for the environment because less of these materials end up in landfills. It also uses fewer natural resources, such as oil for making plastic.

SOLIDS, LIQUIDS, AND GASES

Materials can exist in different states. They can be solids, liquids, or gases.

SOLIDS

- ★ Examples of solid materials include wood, rock, and ice.
- ★ Solids have a fixed shape.
- ★ They only change shape if a force is applied to them.
- ★ Solids always take up the same amount of space.

LIQUIDS

- ★ Examples of liquids include water, milk, and oil.
- ★ Liquids change shape to take the shape of the container they are in.
- ★ They can flow.
- ★ Liquids always take up the same amount of space.

GASES

- ★ Examples of gases include water vapor, oxygen, and carbon dioxide.
- ★ Gases can move around freely.
- ★ They will escape from any open container.
- ★ Gases can change the amount of space they take up and expand or shrink to fill any container.

PARTICLES

Every object is made up of tiny particles. The way in which these particles are arranged determines whether the object is a solid, a liquid, or a gas.

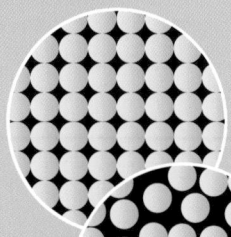

SOLID

In a solid, the particles are fixed together and can't move around.

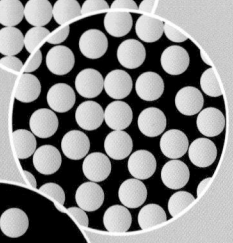

LIQUID

In a liquid, the particles can move around each other, but they can't move closer together or farther apart.

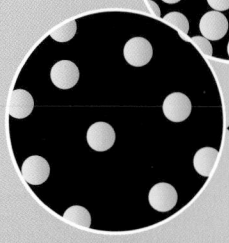

GAS

In a gas, the particles can move freely in any direction, and can move closer together or farther apart.

CHANGING STATES

Heating or cooling can make a material change state.

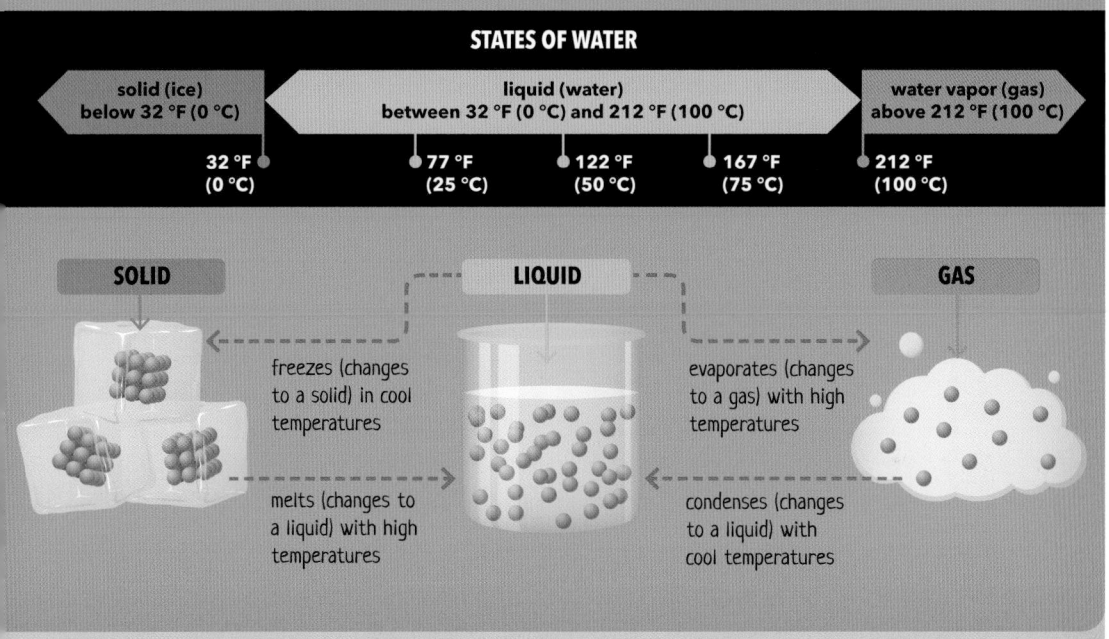

BACK AND FORTH

Some changes in state are reversible. If the temperature is changed, the object will return to its original state. For example, if you apply heat to chocolate, it melts and turns from a solid to a liquid. However, if the liquid chocolate cools down, it turns back into a solid.

Other changes are irreversible. For example, if you bake (heat) liquid cake mix, it forms a solid cake. The solid cake can't be turned back into liquid cake mix by cooling it down.

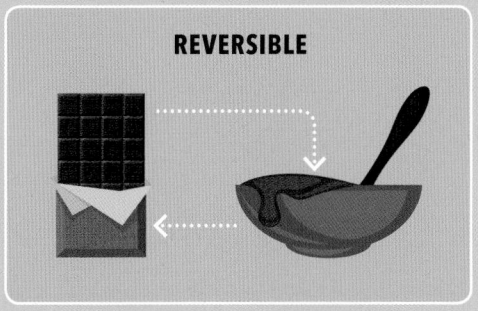

GO QUIZ YOURSELF!

52 What is a human-made material?

53 Name two properties of metal.

54 What does it mean to conduct heat?

55 What is plastic usually made from?

56 Which material is transparent, waterproof, and often strong?

57 What is the environmental problem of plastics and other durable human-made materials?

58 Name one benefit of recycling.

59 Which state of matter has a fixed shape?

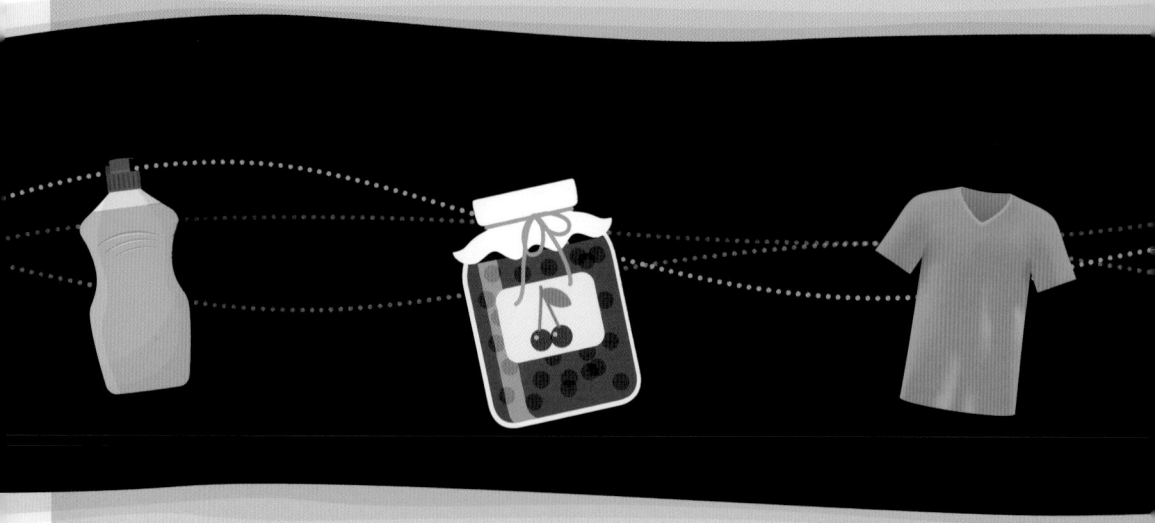

→ **60** How do you make a solid change shape?

61 Which state of matter can change the amount of space it takes up?

62 What tiny things are all objects made up of?

63 How do particles in a liquid behave?

64 If heat is applied to a solid, which state does it change into?

65 What is evaporation?

66 At which temperature does water change from liquid to solid?

67 Give an example of a reversible change.

68 What is an irreversible change?

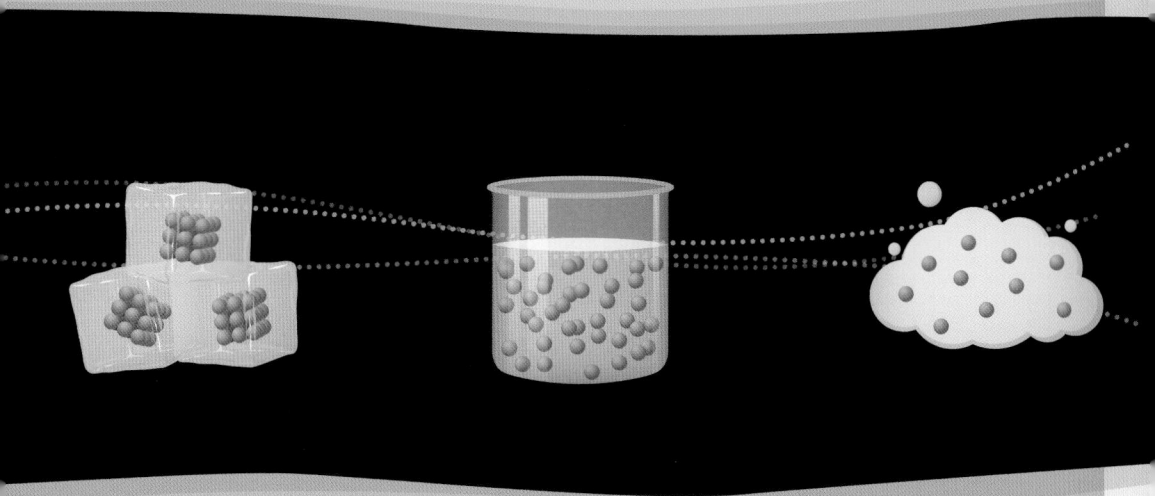

LIVING THINGS

Plants and animals are living things. They have seven main features in common, but they are different in other ways.

ALL LIVING THINGS:

MOVE (change position)

ANIMALS

Some animals move very quickly, while others move much more slowly.

They can move in different ways, such as running, jumping, flying, and swimming.

PLANTS

Plant roots stay in one place, but their stem and leaves grow very slowly toward the Sun.

Young sunflowers can move their flowers to face the Sun.

REPRODUCE (create new living things)

Some animals give birth to live young, while others lay eggs that their young hatch out of.

Most plants **reproduce** using seeds that grow into new plants (see pages 32-33).

SENSE CHANGES IN THE ENVIRONMENT AND REACT TO THEM

Animals use their senses to respond to their environment.

Their five main senses are hearing, sight, smell, touch, and taste.

Plants are sensitive to light and grow toward it.

Some carnivorous plants are touch-sensitive. They snap their leaves shut to trap prey (see page 32).

GROW (get larger)

Most animals are born small and grow into a larger adult size.

Some animals change their shape entirely when they become adults. For example, caterpillars turn into butterflies.

Most plants grow from seeds into small seedlings, then continue to grow larger.

TAKE IN NUTRIENTS

Animals get nutrients by eating other living things.

Some (herbivores) eat plants, while others (carnivores) eat other animals.

Omnivores eat plants and other animals.

Plants make their own food from sunlight, carbon dioxide, and water through a process called **photosynthesis**.

They also need nutrients, which most plants absorb from the soil.

RESPIRE (breathe, or get energy from food)

Animals require oxygen to release energy from food.

Many animals breathe air to get oxygen into their bodies. This oxygen is used to release energy from food. The oxygen reacts with glucose in food to release energy.

Some water animals, such as fish, have gills that absorb oxygen from water.

Plants need oxygen to get energy from the food they produce.

They absorb oxygen from the air through holes in their leaves.

EXCRETE (release waste products)

Animals release waste gases, such as carbon dioxide, by breathing out.

Other waste products are excreted in urine and feces.

Waste gases and unwanted water are released from plants through tiny holes in their leaves.

OTHER LIVING THINGS

Fungi and bacteria aren't plants or animals. They are their own types of living things.

Mushrooms and toadstools are both examples of fungi. They don't produce their own food like plants do. They get their nutrients from other plants or animals, often dead ones.

Bacteria are very small organisms that only have one cell. Some carry out photosynthesis like plants, while others eat other organisms.

PLANTS

There are many different shapes and sizes of plants on Earth. People depend on plants for food, oxygen, and as a key part of all natural habitats.

FLOWERS, FRUIT, AND SEEDS

Flowering plants reproduce by producing flowers, fruit, and seeds. First, they grow bright, colorful flowers that are pollinated (fertilized) by insects or the wind. The fruit that grows from a pollinated flower contains the seeds. Animals and the wind help to carry the seeds to new areas where they grow into new plants.

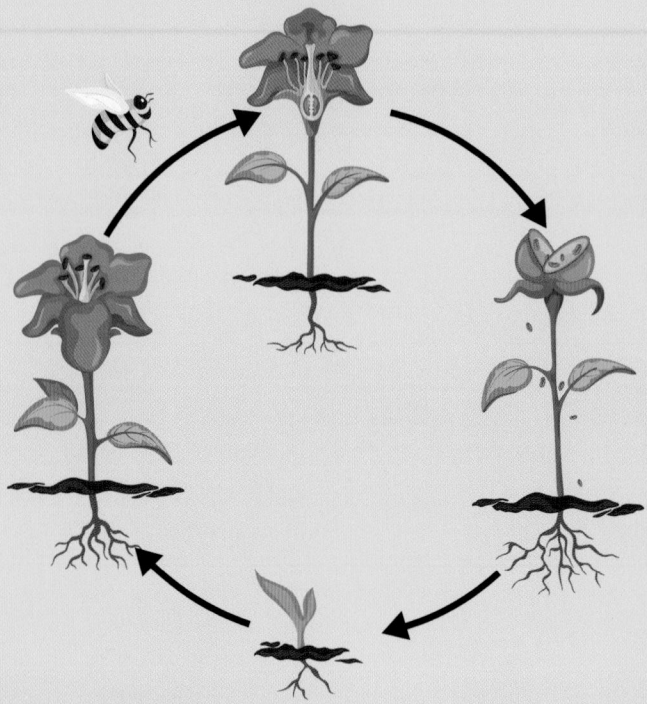

WEIRD AND WONDERFUL PLANTS

The Venus flytrap catches small insects and spiders in its leaves and digests them.

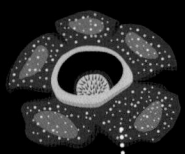

The rafflesia flower is the largest flower in the world, measuring up to 3 feet (1 m) in diameter. It smells like rotting flesh to attract insects, which will pollinate the flower!

Redwood trees are the tallest trees in the world, reaching heights of 377 feet (115 m). This is taller than the Statue of Liberty!

HOW PLANTS GROW

Seeds need to be in a warm, wet environment to germinate (start to grow).

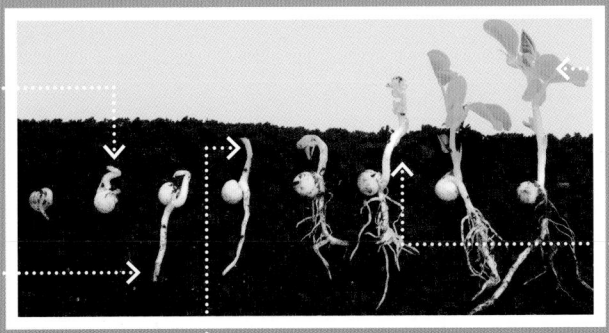

1. First, the seed case breaks open.
2. The roots begin to grow downward.
3. A shoot starts growing upward.
4. Eventually, the shoot breaks through the soil and continues to grow up toward the light.
5. Above ground, the stem and leaves grow out of the shoot.

TREES THROUGH THE YEAR

Deciduous trees look different throughout the year. The leaves of deciduous trees turn yellow, orange, and red in autumn, then start to fall off. They are bare in winter. These trees regrow their leaves in spring. Evergreen trees do not change color. They lose and regrow their leaves gradually throughout the year.

Scientists managed to grow a plant from a 32,000-year-old seed that had been buried by a squirrel and covered in ice!

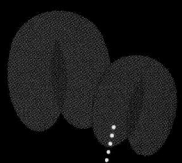

The coco de mer is the largest seed in the world! This giant seed can measure 20 inches (51 cm) in diameter and weigh up to 55 pounds (25 kg)! It comes from a type of palm tree found on the Seychelles islands in the Indian Ocean.

GO QUIZ YOURSELF!

69 How many features do living things have in common?

70 How do plants move?

71 Name two ways that animals reproduce.

72 What are the five main animal senses?

73 What is photosynthesis?

74 How do animals get oxygen for respiration?

75 How do plants release waste gases and unwanted water?

76 Which group of living things does the mushroom belong to?

77 Name something that helps to pollinate flowers.

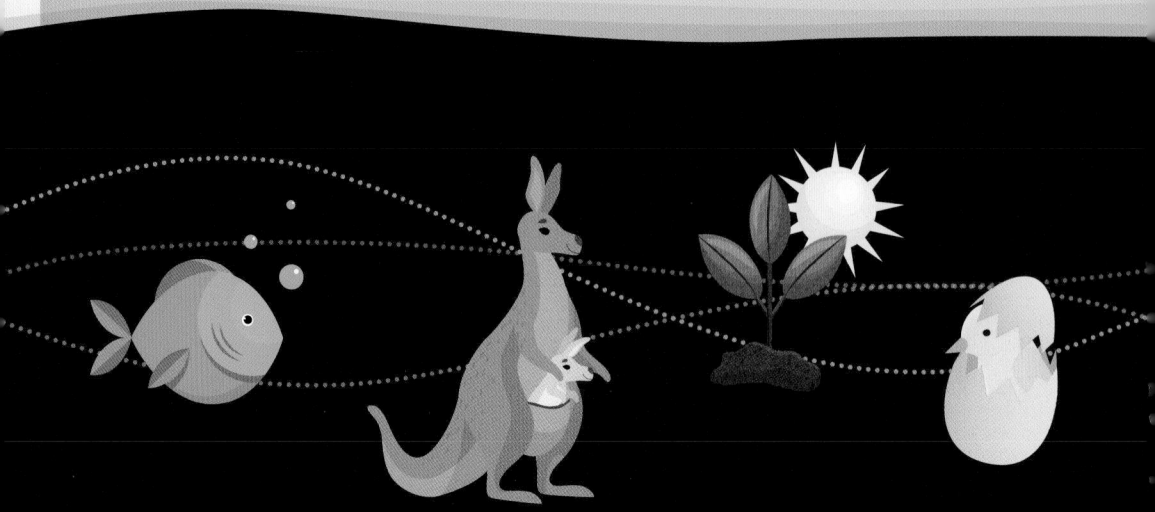

78 What happens after a flower is pollinated?

79 What kind of environment do seeds need to germinate?

80 What happens to deciduous trees in autumn?

81 What is an evergreen tree?

82 Which plant catches small insects and spiders?

83 What is the largest flower in the world?

84 What are the tallest trees in the world?

85 How much can a coco de mer seed weigh?

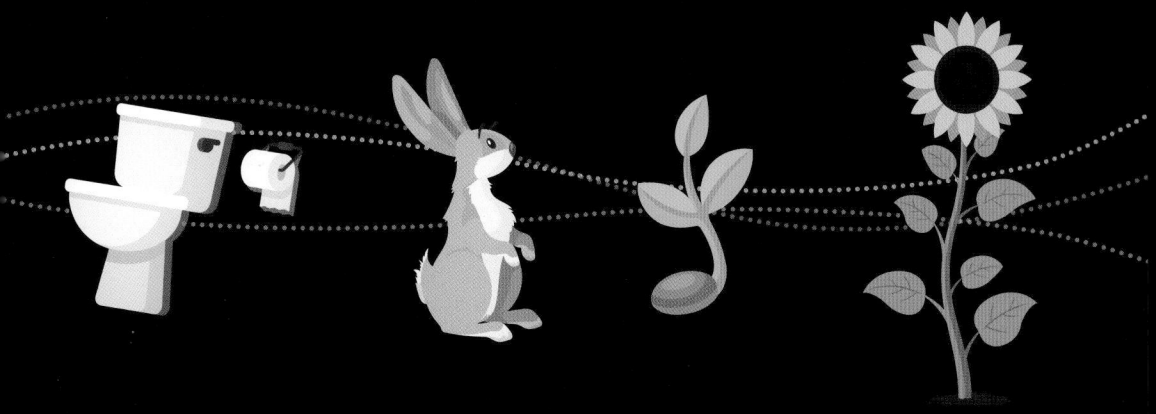

ANCIENT SCIENCE

In the past, ancient civilizations tried to understand the world around them. Some of their theories were correct, while others we now know were incorrect. They also designed incredible inventions that changed society and helped create the world we live in today.

PREHISTORIC PEOPLE

Several important inventions revolutionized prehistoric times. When people learned how to work with bronze and iron, they were able to replace their stone, wood, and bone tools with superior metal tools. This made tasks, such as farming and construction, much easier.

MAKING BRONZE

Metalworking is an ancient technique. Some metalworking today is still done in this way.

To make bronze, copper and tin are melted together.

The liquid bronze is poured into a mold in the shape of the tool or part that is needed.

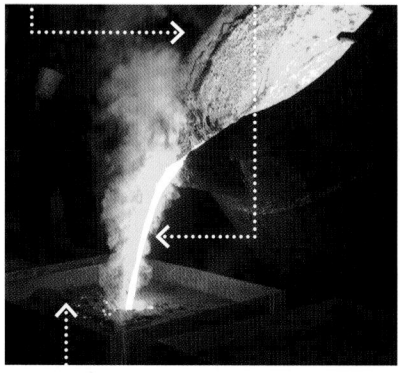

The liquid bronze is left to cool into a solid in the mold.

ANCIENT CHINA

Some of the most important inventions came from ancient China. In the second century CE, paper was invented in China. From there, it spread slowly across the planet, changing society forever. The ancient Chinese also invented gunpowder, which they used in weapons. They also used gunpowder to make the world's first fireworks!

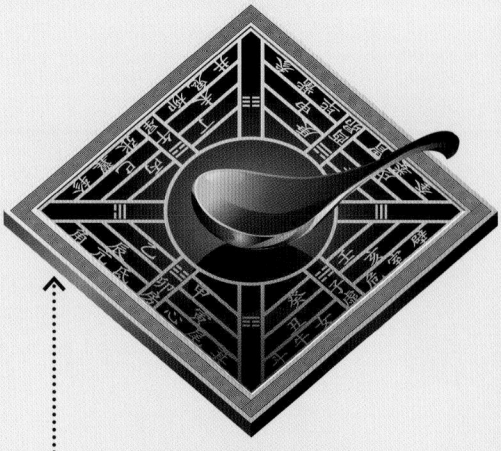

This is an ancient Chinese compass—the first magnetic compass to be invented. The spoon in the center was made of a magnetic material.

ANCIENT GREEKS

The ancient Greeks were very interested in studying the natural world and trying to understand it. They had advanced knowledge of math, geometry, and astronomy. Some amazing ancient Greek inventions include an early form of the alarm clock, which was powered by water, and the Archimedes screw, which is a mechanical way of transporting water.

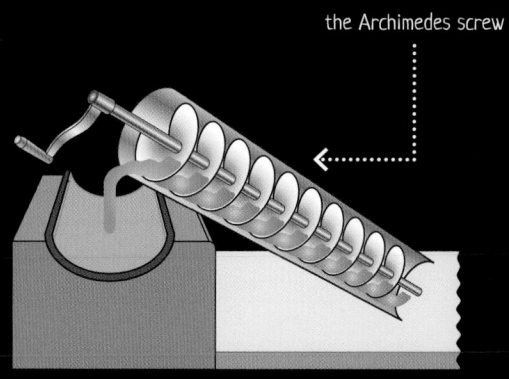

ISLAMIC SCIENTISTS

Scientists in the early Islamic civilization translated many scientific texts from the ancient Greeks and the ancient Romans. They studied these ancient ideas, then developed them further, based on their own research!

Early Islamic doctors wrote many advanced medical texts about the human body.

New surgical instruments were invented by the surgeon Al-Zahrawi. Some of his inventions are still used today, such as the syringe and forceps.

New fields of study, such as chemistry and algebra, were introduced.

One scientist, Abbas ibn Firnas, was even reported to have made a functional flying machine!

The scientist Ibn al-Haytham is the first to correctly explain how vision works.

AMAZING INVENTIONS

Scientists and engineers have created incredible machines that help to make everyday life easier, and improve our understanding of science.

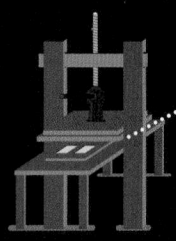

1450

Johannes Gutenberg designed the printing press. Before the printing press, everything was written by hand, which was very slow. Printed materials, such as scientific research and theories, could be created and shared much more quickly and easily with a wider range of people across different countries.

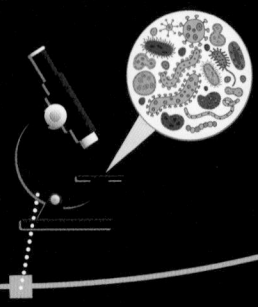

1590

The first compound microscope was invented by Dutch glasses makers Hans and Zacharias Janssen. Scientists were able to see objects in close detail for the first time. This gave them a look at a whole new miniature world.

1843

Ada Lovelace designed the first computer program, based on Babbage's Analytical Engine.

1834

Charles Babbage created the Analytical Engine–a type of mechanical computer.

1864

The first bicycle with pedals was created. Before that, people had to push bicycles forward with their legs! Adding pedals allowed cyclists to travel faster and use less energy.

1903

The Wright brothers took the first airplane flight. This form of transportation became safer and more popular over time and is now used to transport millions of people around the world every day.

1876

Alexander Graham Bell demonstrated his new invention–the telephone. The telephone revolutionized communication, allowing people to quickly contact each other across great distances.

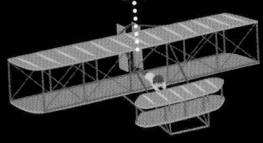

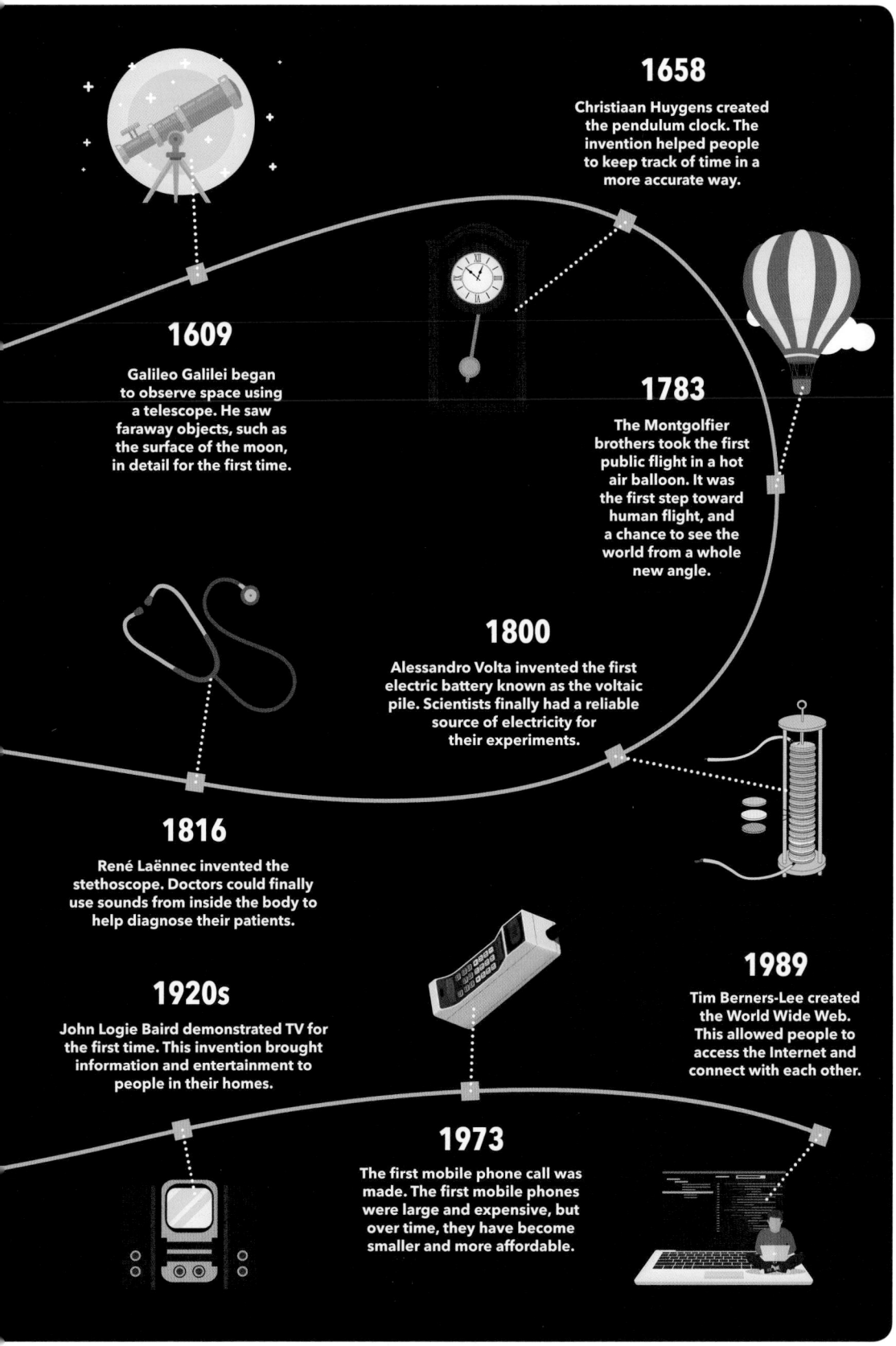
1658
Christiaan Huygens created the pendulum clock. The invention helped people to keep track of time in a more accurate way.
1609
Galileo Galilei began to observe space using a telescope. He saw faraway objects, such as the surface of the moon, in detail for the first time.
1783
The Montgolfier brothers took the first public flight in a hot air balloon. It was the first step toward human flight, and a chance to see the world from a whole new angle.
1800
Alessandro Volta invented the first electric battery known as the voltaic pile. Scientists finally had a reliable source of electricity for their experiments.
1816
René Laënnec invented the stethoscope. Doctors could finally use sounds from inside the body to help diagnose their patients.
1920s
John Logie Baird demonstrated TV for the first time. This invention brought information and entertainment to people in their homes.
1989
Tim Berners-Lee created the World Wide Web. This allowed people to access the Internet and connect with each other.
1973
The first mobile phone call was made. The first mobile phones were large and expensive, but over time, they have become smaller and more affordable.

GO QUIZ YOURSELF!

86 How did metalworking make life easier for prehistoric people?

87 Which two metals are melted together to make bronze?

88 When was paper invented?

89 Name two uses for gunpowder in ancient China.

90 Which civilization invented the first magnetic compass?

91 What powered the alarm clock designed by the ancient Greeks?

92 What was the Archimedes screw?

93 Name a surgical instrument invented by the early Islamic surgeon Al-Zahrawi.

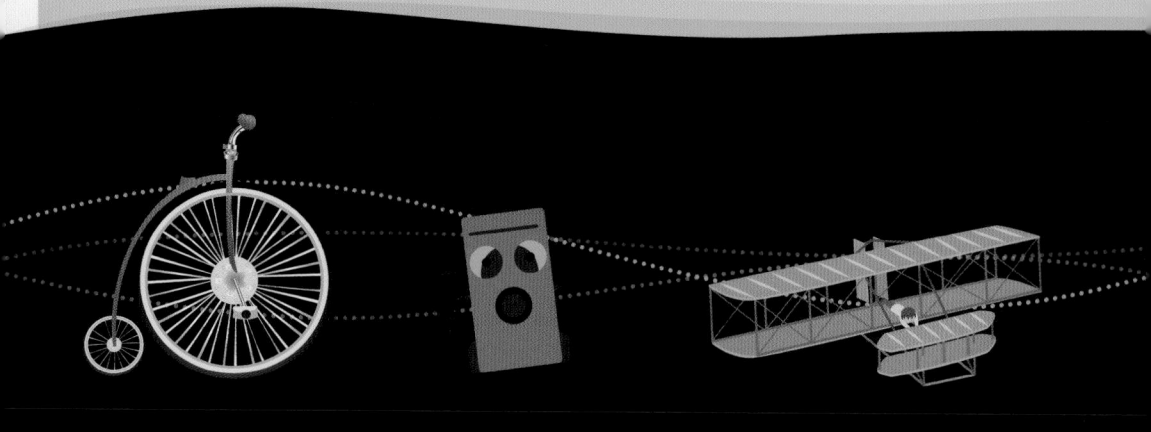

94 What did Galileo Galilei observe with his telescope?

95 What was the voltaic pile?

96 Which vehicle did the Montgolfier brothers fly for the first time in 1783?

97 Who designed the first computer program?

98 How did adding pedals to bicycles help cyclists?

99 What did Alexander Graham Bell invent?

100 In which decade did John Logie Baird demonstrate TV for the first time?

101 When was the first mobile phone call made?

102 Who created the World Wide Web?

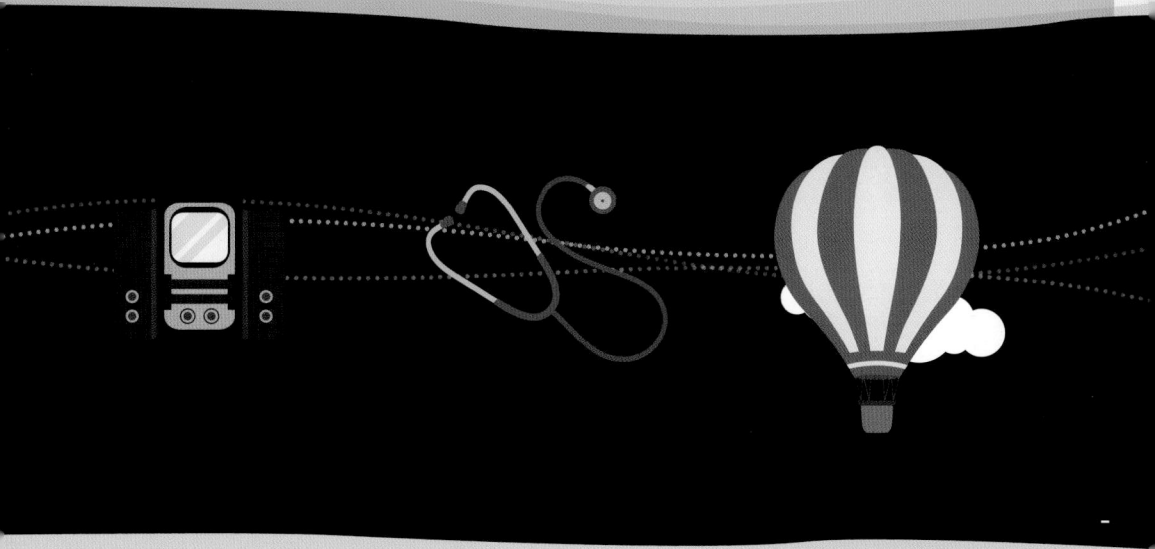

THE FUTURE OF SCIENCE

The scientists of today are working hard on the breakthroughs and inventions of the future. In our lifetime, we will probably see many incredible discoveries that will make life easier and help us to understand science better.

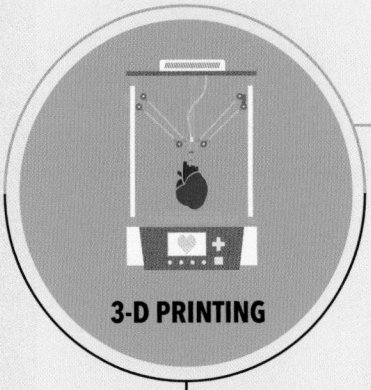

3-D PRINTING

NOW

With a 3-D printer, you can print a 3-D model of anything you want! This technology is already in use and is particularly helpful in hard-to-reach places, such as space or Antarctica, as it can be used to create tools or machine parts on the spot!

THE FUTURE

Scientists are currently researching other uses for 3-D printers, including printing skin and other body tissue using cells. Soon, they might even be able to print whole organs, such as hearts, for transplants.

SUSTAINABLE SOLUTIONS

NOW

We are becoming more and more conscious of our negative impact on the planet. Scientists are working hard to find ways to reduce the damage that we do. Some current solutions are creating fuels from waste, designing **biodegradable** alternatives to plastic, and making artificial meat rather than raising animals on farms.

THE FUTURE

Scientists will continue to come up with solutions to help the environment. These could be new, cleaner fuels, or ways of removing plastic from the ocean. A major focus is to find ways of reducing the greenhouse effect, and therefore global warming, by removing excess carbon dioxide from the atmosphere.

ARTIFICIAL INTELLIGENCE

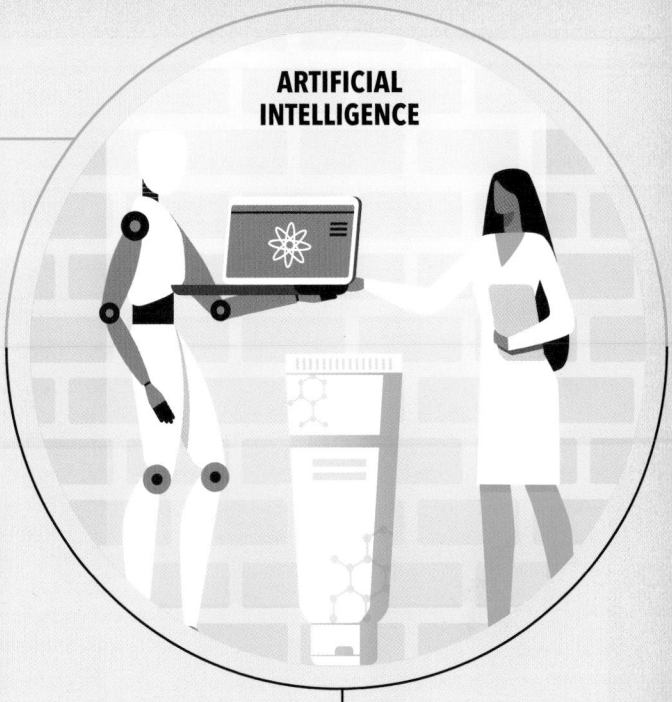

NOW

We already use robots for simple, repetitive tasks in factories and warehouses. However, computer scientists have always been fascinated by the idea of artificial intelligence. They have been able to develop highly complex robots that can have sophisticated interactions with people, as well as solve logical puzzles that would be very hard for humans to do.

THE FUTURE

As scientists continue to study artificial intelligence, robots will continue to become more and more sophisticated and complex. Perhaps robots will be the scientists of the future someday!

QUIZ TIME!

After you've finished testing yourself, why not use this book to make a quiz to test your friends and family? You could take questions from each section to make different rounds, or mix and match across the book for a general knowledge science quiz. You can even make up your own quiz questions! Use these future-of-science facts to get you started. For example, **"How is 3D printing used in space?"** or **"What kinds of tasks are robots used for?"**

ANSWERS

1 The science of life and living things, or plants, animals, and the human body
2 Physics
3 Because gravity pulls on the pancake batter evenly, forming it into a circle
4 The scorpion
5 An object that gives off light
6 Vampire squid, fireflies, anglerfish, crystal jellyfish, some millipedes (and scorpions)
7 Opaque
8 When a translucent or opaque object blocks light
9 Black
10 Because sunlight reflects off tiny particles in the air and scatters mostly blue light across the sky
11 Low-pitched
12 Dogs
13 Decibels
14 60 decibels
15 The eruption of the Krakatoa volcano in 1883
16 Because the walls of a tunnel are hard and reflect sounds, creating echoes
17 A system in which ships use echoes to find objects underwater
18 Light, sound, heat, movement, electrical, or chemical
19 Chemical energy
20 Electrical energy is converted into heat energy
21 Movement energy and heat energy
22 Moving water spins a turbine, which powers a generator that creates electricity
23 A gas produced by burning fossil fuels, which gathers in the atmosphere and traps heat from the Sun near Earth's surface
24 Asthma, certain types of cancer
25 2 °F (just over 1 °C)
26 Current and static
27 Lightbulb, motor, buzzer, battery, wire, or switch
28 Electricity does not flow around the circuit
29 Plastic, wood, glass, rubber
30 Static electricity
31 16.73 seconds
32 Lightning
33 To send messages to and from the brain or to make the heart beat
34 The electric eel
35 Gravity
36 Heavy objects
37 The force that acts on an object when it moves against another object
38 Because there is very little friction
39 It slows the object down
40 Having a smooth shape
41 Horizontal wings
42 Because the weight of the boat pushing down is balanced by the upthrust (pushing force) of the water
43 It will move in the direction of the greater force
44 Iron, steel, nickel, or cobalt
45 The two ends of a magnet
46 They will repel
47 The area around a magnet that is affected by its magnetism
48 Because it has magnetic materials, such as iron and nickel, in its core
49 A bird
50 The magnets hold the train above the tracks, which reduces friction so the train can move faster
51 To store data
52 A material made by people using natural resources
53 Strong, hard, shiny, conducts electricity, conducts heat, often magnetic
54 Let heat pass through
55 Chemicals found in natural gas and oil
56 Glass
57 They won't decompose for hundreds or even thousands of years, so they can pollute natural areas
58 Fewer objects end up in landfills and fewer resources are used to create new materials
59 Solid
60 By applying a force to it
61 Gas
62 Particles

63 In a liquid, the particles can move around each other, but they can't move closer together or farther apart
64 Liquid
65 When heat is applied to a liquid and it changes into a gas
66 32 °F (0 °C)
67 Chocolate melting from a solid to a liquid
68 When something changes state, but can't return to its original state
69 Seven
70 Their stem and leaves grow slowly toward the Sun
71 Give birth to live young or lay eggs that young hatch out of
72 Hearing, sight, smell, touch, and taste
73 The process in which plants use sunlight, carbon dioxide, and water to produce their own food
74 They breathe in air, which contains oxygen, or absorb oxygen from water using gills
75 Through tiny holes in their leaves
76 Fungi
77 Insects or the wind
78 It produces a fruit, which contains seeds
79 Warm and wet
80 Their leaves turn yellow, orange, and red and start to fall off
81 A tree that doesn't change color in fall, and loses and regrows its leaves gradually throughout the year
82 The Venus flytrap
83 The rafflesia flower
84 Redwood trees
85 Up to 55 lbs (25 kg)
86 Metal tools made farming and construction much easier
87 Copper and tin
88 The second century CE
89 Weapons and fireworks
90 The ancient Chinese
91 Water
92 A mechanical way of transporting water
93 The syringe or forceps
94 Objects in space, such as the surface of the moon
95 The first electric battery
96 The hot air balloon
97 Ada Lovelace
98 They could travel faster and use less energy
99 The telephone
100 The 1920s
101 1973
102 Tim Berners-Lee

HOW WELL DID YOU DO?

100-102	QUIZMASTER
75-99	QUIZTASTIC
50-74	QUIZ ON
25-49	QUIZLING
0-24	QUIZ IT AGAIN

GLOSSARY

amplitude The height of a wave

artificial intelligence Developing computers and robots that have intelligence similar to that of a human

atoms The smallest units that an element can be divided into

biodegradable Something that breaks down naturally without harming the environment

circuit Electrical systems made up of electrical sources and wires

components Elements in a circuit, such as lightbulbs or motors

conductors Materials that electricity or heat can pass through

elements Substances that can't be broken down into other substances

global warming The increase in temperature on Earth

gravity A force that pulls things toward each other

greenhouse gases Gases that gather in Earth's atmosphere, trapping heat from the Sun close to Earth's surface

insulators Materials that electricity or heat can't pass through

magnetic field The area affected by a magnet's magnetism

navigation Finding the right direction to travel in

particles Very small pieces of something

photosynthesis The process by which plants make their own food

reproduce To produce young animals or new plants

resistance Friction that works on objects moving through air or water

states of matter Whether something is a solid, a liquid, or a gas

streamlined Designed in a way that makes it easier to move through air or water

turbine A type of machine in which liquids or gases power a wheel that generates electricity

vibrate To shake continuously and rapidly

volume How loud or quiet a sound is

FURTHER INFORMATION

BOOKS

Claybourne, Anna. Recreate Scientific Discoveries series. Crabtree Publishing, 2019.

Inventions That Shaped the Modern World series. Crabtree Publishing, 2014.

Spilsbury, Richard. *Investigating Science Challenges*. Crabtree Publishing, 2018.

WEBSITES

www.britannica.com/story/history-of-technology-timeline
Explore a timeline of some of the greatest inventions of all time.

www.coolkidfacts.com/electricity-facts
Discover some "shocking" facts about electricity!

www.bbc.co.uk/bitesize/articles/zsgwwxs
Learn more about the states of matter—solids, liquids, and gases.

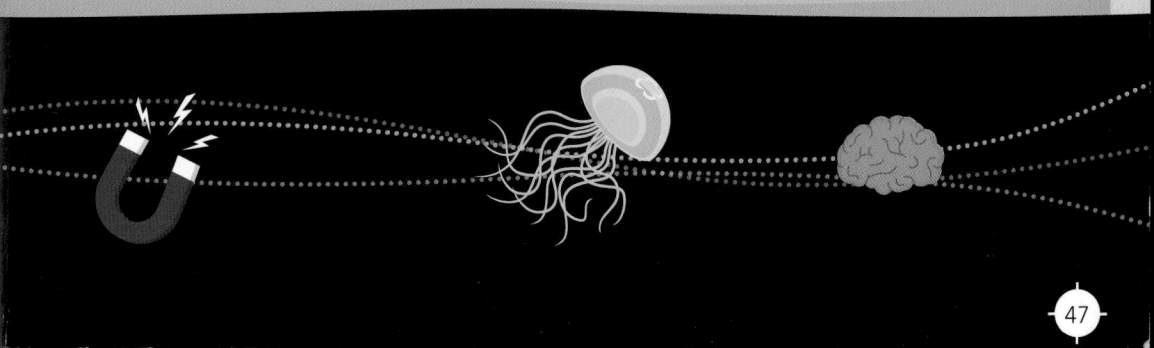

INDEX

3-D printing 42

ancient China 36
ancient Greece 37
animals 4, 5, 6, 8, 15, 21, 30–31, 32, 42
artificial intelligence 43

biology 4

chemistry 4, 37
circuits 14

early Islamic civilization 37
electricity 5, 6, 12, 13, 14–15, 24, 39
energy 4, 12–13, 14, 31

flowers 30, 32
forces 4, 5, 18–19, 20, 21, 26
friction 18, 19, 21
fruit 32

gases 5, 13, 26, 27, 31
global warming 13
gravity 5, 18

inventions 36, 37, 38–39

light 5, 6–7, 12, 30, 31, 33
lightning 15
liquids 4, 5, 26, 27, 36
living things 4, 30–31

magnets 4, 20–21, 24, 36
materials 6, 7, 14, 15, 20, 24–25, 26, 27, 36

particles 5, 7, 15, 26
physics 4
plants 4, 5, 12, 24, 30, 31, 32–33
prehistory 36

recycling 25
resistance 19

shadows 7
solids 5, 26, 27, 36
sound 5, 8–9, 12, 21
sustainable science 42

water 5, 7, 9, 13, 14, 19, 24, 26, 27, 31, 37
waves 4, 5, 8, 9

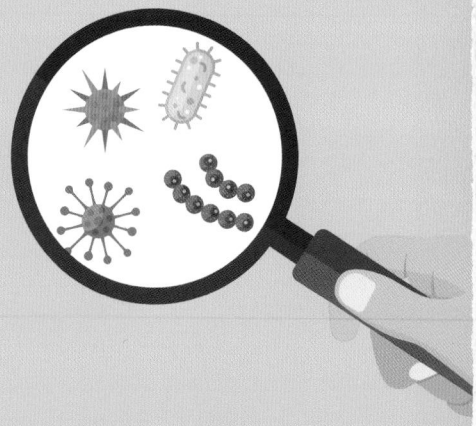